ECOLOGY ALERT!

Coasts

John Baines

RAINTREE
STECK-VAUGHN
PUBLISHERS
A Steck-Vaughn Company

Austin, Texas

Ecology Alert!

Coasts	**Farming**
Communities	**Transportation**
Energy	**Rivers**

Cover: Cleaning up a beach and a seabird after an oil spill at sea
Title page: Garbage from the sea washed up on a beach
Contents page: Cape Hangklip, South Africa

Published by Raintree Steck-Vaughn Publishers, an imprint of Steck-Vaughn Company

Library of Congress Cataloging-in-Publication Data
Baines, John.
Coasts / John Baines.
    p.   cm.—(Ecology Alert)
Includes bibliographical references and index.
Summary: Describes different types of coasts, the animals and plants they support, the resources they provide for humans, how they are endangered, and how they can be protected. Includes case studies and activities.
ISBN 0-8172-5370-X
1. Coasts—Juvenile literature.
2. Coasts—Study and teaching—Activity programs —Juvenile literature.
3. Coasts—Environmental conditions—Juvenile literature.
[1. Coasts.]
I. Title. II. Series.
GB453.B35   2000
333.91'716—dc21   98-25830

Printed in Italy. Bound in the United States.
1 2 3 4 5 6 7 8 9 0 03 02 01 00 99

Picture acknowledgments
Aerofilms Limited 7; Axiom Photographic Agency (Jim Holmes) 25; Chapel Studios (Zul Mukhida) 6; James Davis Travel Photography 10, 17; Ecoscene (Wayne Lawler) 13; Robert Estall Photo Library 18; Eye Ubiquitous (Tim Hawkins) 1, (M. Allwood-Coppin) 3, 8–9, (Pauline Thornton) 5, (Bob Gibbons) 8, (Paul Seheult) 26, (Paul Thompson) 28; Getty Images (Art Wolfe) 4–5, (David Olsen) 19, (Nigel Press) 20, (David Woodfall) 22; Horsehead Wetlands Center, 27 (both); Impact Photos (Javed A. Jafferji) 12, (Simon Grosset) 14, (Mark Henley) 15, (Piers Cavendish) 21, (Rives/Cedri) 23; RSPB Images 11; Topham Picturepoint 16, 24.

Contents

Where the Land Meets the Sea

The surface of the earth is covered by land and water. Sea covers 70 percent of the earth. The land covers only 30 percent. Where the land and the sea meet is called the coast.

Types of coasts

There are many different types of coasts. In some places there are bays and beaches where soft rocks are worn away by the waves breaking on them. People enjoy beaches, especially in warm countries, for games, swimming, and sunbathing.

Rocky outcrops may form headlands and cliffs where seabirds make their nests. The steep slopes of the cliffs make them unsuitable for buildings.

Bora Bora atoll is a tiny island in the middle of the Pacific Ocean. It is ringed by a long, sandy beach.

Coasts and rivers

An estuary is where the mouth of a river meets the sea. At the edges of the river, the land is covered and uncovered by the water as the tides go in and out. Plants may grow on this land, or the land may be mudflats. There is plenty of food in estuaries for plants, fish, and birds.

Other rivers form deltas when they reach the sea. These rivers carry fine soil, called silt, in their water. When the river meets the sea, the silt falls to the bottom and gradually builds up to form rich soil. Deltas are important places for farming.

Tides

Tides are the rise and fall of the sea. They are caused by the pull of the moon's gravity on the water surrounding the earth.

High tide is when the water comes up to the highest point on the shore.

Low tide is when the water goes down to its lowest point. Most places have roughly two high tides and two low tides every 24 hours.

▲ Cliffs are a common type of coast. Some are so steep that only plants and birds can live there.

Coastlines are always changing, because water and wind work on them all the time. Sometimes an entire beach can be washed away in a big storm. In other places, bays or harbors can be filled up with silt to form more land.

The importance of coasts

Coasts cover only a small area of land. They are home to many plants, birds, and animals. They can be areas of great natural beauty. But all over the world, coasts are also where most people live.

Coasts can be changed by wind, waves, and what people do to them.

Activity

The nearest coast

Find a map of your area or your country. Find out where your home or school is on the map. Then locate the coast that is nearest to you and look at it on the map.

- How far away is the coast from your home or school?
- What is there: a town, beach, port, or cliffs?
- Can you tell if many people live there?
- Is the land hilly or flat?
- Are there roads or railroads?
- Are there any rivers, bays, inlets, or islands?

Using other sources of information, such as books, newspapers, tourist guides, or even visiting it yourself, find out more about this coastal area.

Lost to the Sea

Dunwich is a small village in Suffolk, on the east coast of Great Britain. Today, only about 130 people live there, but over the centuries it has been a Roman fort, the capital of a Saxon kingdom, and a busy port. By the eleventh century, Dunwich was the tenth largest town in England. It had many large churches, hospitals, public buildings, and even a mint, for making money. The people who lived there were rich from trading, shipbuilding, and fishing.

However, by the fourteenth century, the harbor started filling up with silt, and the cliffs were being washed away by the sea. Violent storms caused more damage, and gradually hundreds of houses and other buildings fell into the sea.

Now the coast is about 2,625 ft. (800 m) farther inland than it used to be. Some people say that if you listen carefully, you can hear a church bell ringing beneath the waves!

The ruined building in the lower part of the photograph is all that remains of old Dunwich.

 Animals and Plants

Many different kinds of plants and animals live on coasts. Some of these plants and animals live on the land, others belong to the sea, and a few are able to live on the land and in the sea.

Puffins are birds that spend much of the year at sea, catching and eating fish. But during the breeding season they nest in burrows along the shore and feed their young with fish they catch close to the shore. Coastal cliffs are usually covered with seabirds during the breeding season.

◀ **Sea lions live on the coast of the Galapagos Islands, to the west of South America.**

Between the tides

The shoreline, between high and low tide, is also an important place for wildlife. Plants and animals that live there are able to survive periods in and out of the water. Shellfish are really sea creatures, but some are able to survive for a while without water. This is because they have hard shells and can clamp themselves tightly on to rocks. That way they do not dry out when the tide goes out and leaves them uncovered.

Mudflats and rock pools that are exposed at low tide provide plenty of food for birds. It is quite common to see huge flocks of birds moving in and out with the tide and digging up food with their beaks.

Mud and food
Estuaries provide food for millions of birds. About 35 cu.ft. (1 cu. m) of mud from an estuary contains the same amount of food energy as 12 chocolate bars.

The sea is a rich feeding ground for seabirds called gannets in South Africa. In between catching fish, they rest in huge groups on the land.

Estuaries

The areas of river estuaries that are affected by the tides are very rich in wildlife. Found here are plants and animals from both the fresh water of the river and the salty water of the sea. There is plenty of food because the river carries it from inland. Because the water is usually shallow, sunlight reaches the bottom. This means that plants can grow easily.

These conditions make estuaries ideal breeding places for fish. Many fish caught at sea began their life in the shallow waters of estuaries.

Mangrove trees grow along coasts and river estuaries in warm countries. These golden mustard rays are found in the mangrove swamps of Ecuador in South America.

Defenses

Nature also provides coastal defenses. Sand dunes protect low-lying land from flooding when there are high tides and storms. Cliffs absorb the energy of huge destructive waves that could easily knock down a house. Reed beds in marshes can even process our pollution so it does not damage the natural environment.

Natural "Service Stations" for Birds

Many kinds of birds migrate. They cover huge distances—sometimes thousands of miles. Like anyone taking a long journey, birds need places to stop, rest, and get some food.

The sanderling is a small gray-and-white bird. You would never know to look at it, but the sanderling is one of nature's extraordinary travelers.

Sanderlings breed in the Arctic, feeding along the shoreline. The Arctic summer is short, and food is available only for a limited time. Then the birds must move away to find food somewhere else. Some of them travel to West Africa, but others fly all the way to the Cape of Good Hope, at the tip of southern Africa.

This is much too far to go all at once, so the sanderlings stop at natural "service stations" along the way, resting before the long flight to their next stopping-off point. The following spring they return, on their way back to the Arctic.

If beaches and estuaries along the route are built over or turned into farmland then these birds—and many others—would suffer from a lack of food. Conservationists in many countries work together to make sure there are regular stopping points for birds that migrate.

Some sanderlings stop off in Great Britain and France. They spend up to five weeks feeding at beaches and estuaries before moving on.

People and Coasts

Humans, like other living creatures, use the resources that nature provides. Coastal areas can be extremely rich in natural resources, and they can support a lot of people. What makes coasts so attractive?

Fish and farming

Coastal regions have always been good places to live because both the water and the land provide food. Many people who live near coasts can fish the waters and farm the land.

Although people still hunt for fish in boats, others keep fish in ponds or underwater cages. People in Southeast Asia have "farmed" fish for hundreds of years. Mud banks built around paddy fields hold in water for growing rice. The paddies are also used to keep fish and ducks for people to eat.

On many coasts today, fish and shrimp farming are big business. Large areas of mangrove forest have been cleared to make way for ponds. On the coasts of colder countries, salmon are grown in cages in the seawater.

Many people who live on coasts catch fish. They can eat the fish themselves or sell them to earn some money.

Shrimp Farming

Tropical shrimp breed off the coast of Ecuador in South America. Although they are expensive to buy, shrimp are popular in restaurants around the world, especially in Europe and the United States.

Fishermen found it hard to catch enough shrimp to meet the demand, so the shrimp are now farmed.

Shrimp larvae are collected from the sea and are grown in the ponds. When they reach full size they can be sold for a lot of money. But it does not take long before problems occur. The ponds become poisoned with shrimp waste and the crowded shrimp catch diseases. Often, the water pumped into the ponds is already polluted.

Large ponds are dug in the coastal mangrove swamps. This destroys the mangrove trees and the places where fish breed and grow.

After a few years most of the ponds cannot be used any more. New ones are dug, farther up the coast. This ruins yet more mangrove swamps and fish habitats. Local fishermen can lose their incomes as a result of the shrimp farming.

Farming on land

The most popular areas of the coast for farming are the level areas where rivers reach the sea, especially river deltas. Deltas are often flooded. This can be very dangerous for the people who live there. However, the floods leave rich silt over the land, making it very fertile, so the soil is good for farming once the water level has gone down.

This part of New Zealand is too mountainous in the center for farming, but has roads and farms near the sea.

Some countries, such as the Netherlands, have made more farmland from the flat land that is uncovered at low tide. Walls, called dykes, are built around the land to keep out the sea. Ditches are then dug for the water to drain into and this water is pumped out into the sea.

Transportation and trade

For thousands of years people almost always traveled across the oceans in ships. When explorers, traders, or settlers went to new countries, the first places they arrived at were coasts.

Coastal ports are still places for trade because most goods, especially bulky ones such as oil or coal, are carried by ships.

Many cities have grown up around natural harbors. These are bays that protect ships from strong winds and high waves. Some of the world's best-known harbor cities include San Francisco, New York, Sydney, Tokyo, and Rio de Janeiro.

Today the land around these harbors has been built over. Docks, warehouses, factories, roads, airports, shopping areas, and houses have been developed to take advantage of the trade. Often, very little of the natural coast remains.

Ships load and unload at ports on coasts. This Japanese ship is being loaded in Hong Kong.

People on the move

With the exception of Antarctica, humans have settled on every continent in the world.

People from Asia migrated to North and South America more than 10,000 years ago. These people gradually developed their own ways of living and customs, and in time became the Inuit, Native Americans, and South American Indians that we know today. These people were followed by settlers from all over Europe, who started arriving in ships beginning in the 1500s.

Many people who went to a new country never moved beyond the coasts where they arrived. Today, these coasts are usually the most developed and heavily populated areas of the country. There is often very little evidence of the first people who lived there.

During the nineteenth and early twentieth centuries, millions of people migrated to settle new countries. These people are arriving in Great Britain from the West Indies in 1958.

Sea, sun, sand, and tourists

Coasts are popular places for people to enjoy themselves swimming, boating, sunbathing, taking part in water sports, or just enjoying the view. Some people travel thousands of miles for a vacation in a warm country.

Coasts in cooler countries are also popular with visitors. People come to see the beautiful scenery and the wildlife and to enjoy the fresh air and open space. Many of these areas have been bought by conservation groups so that they can be taken care of properly and to make them better for both wildlife and visitors.

Places with warm seas and sandy beaches, such as Hawaii, attract millions of visitors every year.

Activity

Vacation watch

Get a vacation brochure from a travel agent, or find a page of vacation advertisements in a newspaper or magazine. On a large map of your chosen country, or the world, stick a colored pin in each vacation area listed. Then answer the following questions:

- Which is the farthest place?
- How far away is it?
- Which is the most frequently listed area or country?
- What percentage of places are on the coast?
- What is the most popular type of coast for vacations?
- What is the main type of transportation used to reach the vacation area?
- Which area would you most like to visit and why?

Coasts in Danger

Coastal areas are not just made up of the land stretching down to the water. They include both the land and the water. Around the world, these areas support about 4.5 billion people.

Coasts everywhere are being harmed by what people are doing, either directly or indirectly. They are most in danger from building, pollution, and a rising sea level. To this list could be added ignorance. Too many people still think coasts are useless wastelands that are made useful only by development, such as building.

We need to learn more about what the damage is, what the consequences are, how the damage is caused, and what we can do to correct the problems.

Some natural areas like this river estuary can look drab and lifeless. But they are often home to all kinds of fish, birds, and tiny sea animals.

Development projects

The more coastal land that is farmed or built on, the less space there is for nature. For some people, changing a drab area of salt marsh and mudflats into farmland, an industrial site, or housing may seem to improve it.

But what are some of the costs? That area may no longer help to prevent flooding or absorb pollution. It may no longer provide food for birds or be a place for fish to breed.

This part of San Diego, California, has been developed with offices, stores, and a marina for boats.

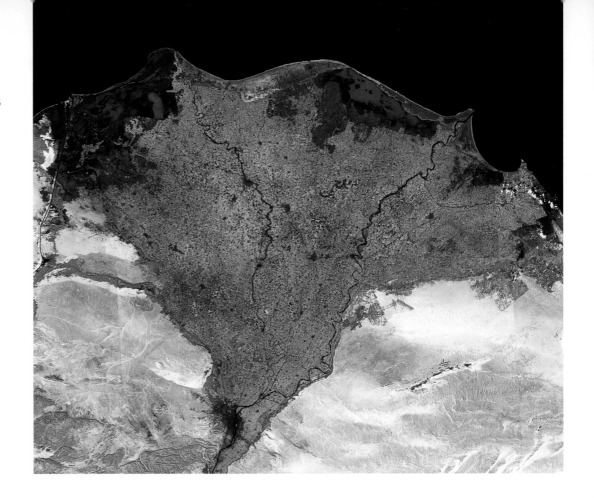

The Nile River in Egypt has a huge delta that spreads over many miles. This photograph was taken from a satellite high above the earth.

Even development a long way inland can have an impact on the coast. In Egypt, the Aswan High Dam was built across the Nile River in 1964. The water in the dam is used for fishing, provides water for farming and electricity, and prevents flooding farther down the Nile.

However, the dam also stops silt carried by the river from reaching the river delta, about 600 mi. (1,000 km) away. The delta is sinking faster than new soil is arriving. To prevent the sea from flooding this area, expensive defenses such as sea walls have to be built. Farmers also find they need to use more fertilizer to produce their crops.

Another side effect was that the amount of fish caught offshore went down from 22,600 tons in 1966 to only 10,300 tons in 1972. This was because nutrients for plants that fish feed on were left behind in the dam instead of flowing down the river and into the sea.

Tourism

Many people like to visit coasts for beaches and beautiful scenery. But coasts can often be overused. Building roads, hotels, and houses along a coast can create more pollution, disturb wildlife, and spoil the way the coasts look. Sometimes even activities such as walking can cause erosion problems.

Pollution

Pollution has become a serious problem along many coasts. People have used the sea as a garbage dump, believing that it was so large that anything put into it would not be noticed once it was washed out to sea.

Untreated sewage is one form of pollution. Many cities around the world pump their sewage straight into the sea faster than the organisms living in the sea can break it down and make it safe.

Coasts can be ruined by too many buildings, roads, and people.

Many chemicals used in homes, offices, factories, and farms are washed into the sea. These damage sea life and sometimes people. For example, the Baltic Sea east of Sweden used to contain many plants and animals. Now, below a depth of 164 ft. (50 m), nothing can live there.

Sewage that is washed up on swimming beaches is unpleasant and unhealthy.

What a load of garbage!

Even on one of the most isolated beaches in the world it is possible to find trash.

Ducie Atoll is a coral atoll in the South Pacific. No one lives there. It is 3,100 mi. (5,000 km) from the nearest continent and 310 mi. (500 km) from the nearest inhabited island, tiny Pitcairn Island. The atoll has no fresh water and so does not attract any shipping. However, in 1991, the following junk was found washed up on the coast:

- **171 glass bottles from 15 countries**
- **113 large and small buoys (sea markers)**
- **74 bottle tops**
- **25 shoes**
- **14 bread and bottle crates**
- **7 food and drink cans**
- **6 fluorescent light tubes**
- **1 toy airplane**
- **2 heads from dolls**
- **2 ballpoint pen tops**

Oil Pollution in the Persian Gulf

Most beaches around the world show some signs of oil pollution. Sometimes huge quantities of oil suddenly hit a coast, such as when an oil tanker accidentally spills its load. These spills cause great damage. However, oil is a natural substance and nature seems to be able to clean it up and recover in time, as long as there is no more pollution.

The countries surrounding the Persian Gulf are the most important oil producers in the world. Much of the oil is taken away through the Gulf in tankers.

During the Gulf War (1990–91), oil storage tanks in Kuwait were deliberately opened by Iraqi soldiers. The oil spread along the coast, forming a huge slick many miles long. As many as 30,000 seabirds may have died immediately.

Many coasts in the Persian Gulf were badly damaged by oil during the Persian Gulf War. A huge cleanup operation was needed, and now the area seems to be recovering.

However, the problem was worse than this. The Gulf coast has salt marshes, mangrove swamps, and coral islands. These are important feeding grounds for millions of migrating birds that pass through there every year. This has also affected the fishing industry. There are now many fewer fish.

Climate change

Coasts around the world are likely to be affected by rising amounts of carbon dioxide (CO_2) in the air. Most of the increase is caused by burning fossil fuels such as oil, coal, and gas. These fuels are used to heat and cool our buildings, generate electricity, make metals, and power vehicles.

Most scientists believe that this extra carbon dioxide is causing the climate to change all over the world. Some countries seem to be getting hotter, while others may be cooling down. It is these changes that will affect the coasts.

Nearly 80 percent of the earth's water is frozen as ice in the Arctic and Antarctic.

If parts of the earth become warmer, glaciers and the ice caps at the North and South poles may melt and become smaller. The extra water in the oceans would cause the general level of the sea to rise, perhaps by as much as 10 ft. (1.8 m) by the middle of the twenty-first century.

Some coastlines would be flooded. The countries with low-lying coasts, such as the Netherlands and Bangladesh, would suffer most. People there must choose whether to build expensive sea defences or give up land to the sea and retreat inland.

If climates change and the sea level rises, wild plants and animals living on coasts might not be able to adapt quickly enough. Marshes and mudflats would be covered by water. Animals would have to go elsewhere for food, or they might even die out altogether.

Floodwater destroys crops in fields, gets into homes, and pollutes drinking water so that it is no longer safe.

Activity

Oil spill

Imagine there has been an oil spill on a coast near you. Here is an experiment to see how you might be able to clean it up.

You will need a large jar with a lid, water, salt, and some motor oil. Fill the jar two-thirds full with water. Add a large spoonful of salt. Stir the water to dissolve the salt.

Pour some oil into the jar so that there is a small drop of oil floating on the top of the water. Put the lid tightly on the jar and shake it well. What happens to the oil? Put a bird's feather into the oil. What happens to the feather?

Try to clean up the oil. Use a spoon, cotton balls, and scraps of fabric. Which method works best?

Protecting Coasts

Coasts are very valuable. They provide a living for more people than the rest of the land on the planet. Coasts are the part of the earth where the most development takes place, and where protection is most needed. How can we make sure that coasts are not all harmed?

The population of Florida grows at the rate of 1,000 people per day. Already almost half of Florida's wetlands have been lost. The loss continues at the rate of about 74 acres (30 ha) per day.

Education

Many people still think of flat coastal areas as wasteland and in need of development. While some building and changes are necessary, it is also important to show people why coastal areas should be protected.

Education programs can help. For example, in Brisbane, Australia, the Queensland Parks and Wildlife Service built a boardwalk through a mangrove area in a suburb of the city. There are noticeboards, with a cartoon character, providing fascinating information about an area that some people thought was a wasteland.

A sign on a beach in Phuket, Thailand. It shows visitors how to prevent damage to the local coral reef.

In many countries, there is now World Wetland Week to teach people about wetlands, including coasts. The first one took place in February 1997. Organizations around the world put on events and exhibitions for people living in or near wetland areas.

▼ Visitors to the Wetlands Center make friends with some of the geese who live there.

CASE STUDY

Protecting Chesapeake Bay

Chesapeake Bay runs along the coast of the states of Maryland and Virginia. It is over 186 mi. (300 km) long. Water from rivers in five states empties into the bay. Fifteen million people live in the region, and many kinds of waste find their way to the coastal water.

The bay has some wonderful places for wildlife, but it has suffered from development and overfishing. The area was famous for its oysters, but numbers are now only 1 percent of what they were in the 1870s. Since 1976, people have tried to protect the area. Laws have been passed to reduce the amount of harmful waste getting into rivers, and catching some types of fish has been banned.

▼ Students use a very fine net to catch tiny organisms living in the water.

The Horsehead Wetlands Center at Grasonville, Maryland, teaches visitors about the coastal wetland habitat and its wildlife. It contains natural areas where people can use huts, towers, and a boardwalk to watch all the different birds and animals. These include songbirds, deer, red foxes, bald eagles, butterflies, hummingbirds, turtles, ducks, herons, and egrets.

Research

We are beginning to understand how nature works in estuaries, salt marshes, and other coastal areas. Scientists are able to give advice about the advantages and disadvantages of developments, and where they will cause the least damage. In some countries, before major building projects are allowed to start, research is carried out to discover how best to protect the environment.

Conservation

Another way to protect an area is to turn it into a nature preserve or conservation area. The area is then kept as natural as possible. People enjoy visiting preserves. Often, where visitors can go and what they can do is carefully controlled so that the wildlife is not disturbed too much.

Coasts are valuable areas in both their natural state and when they have been changed for human use. Building and development are necessary so that people can live, work, and trade. But it would be a disaster if every coastline were developed. There needs to be a balance between people's needs and the natural world.

This beautiful coast attracts many visitors. But the footpaths and cliffs are being eroded. They need to be protected so the area is not spoiled for future visitors.

ACTIVITY

Coast watch

Look at this drawing of an imaginary coastline. It shows many different features.

List what you can find under these headings:
- Natural features, such as cliffsand rock pools.
- Human-made features, such as roads and docks.
- Ways of earning a living, such as fishing and tourism.
- Recreation, such as walking and bird watching.

Which areas do you think should be protected? Can you say why?

Glossary

Absorb To swallow up or take in.

Atoll A ring-shaped coral reef that has a lagoon (a saltwater lake) inside it.

Breed To have children or offspring.

Conservation Looking after natural resources so that they will still be there in the future for people to use.

Conservationists People who practice or carry out conservation.

Continent A very large area of land, such as North America or Asia.

Defense Something that protects against damage or attack.

Delta A fan-shaped area at the mouth of a river where the river splits into many channels before reaching the sea.

Developed When a place is changed by building roads, housing, and factories.

Erosion The wearing away of the earth's surface.

Estuary The mouth of a river at the sea where freshwater meets seawater.

Fertile Something, such as soil, that is rich and productive.

Flood When a lot of water covers land that is normally dry.

Gravity The force of the earth and the moon that pulls objects toward their centers.

Habitat The natural home of a plant or animal.

Larvae The young form of some animals, including insects.

Marsh Low-lying land that is almost always covered by water.

Migrate To move from one place or country to another.

Mint A place where money is made.

Natural resources Materials provided by nature that humans use to survive or to improve their lives.

Organisms Living animals or plants.

Paddy A field where rice is grown with banks around it to hold in water.

Pollution Harmful materials in the environment.

Port A place where ships stop to load or unload goods or people.

Settler Someone who goes to a new place to live.

Sewage Mostly liquid waste that is carried away from homes.

Species A group of plants or animals with similar features.

Tides The rise and fall of the sea on the shore.

Wetland An area of low-lying land that is covered by water for much of the year.

Further Information

Books

Coster, Patience. *Seas and Coasts* (Step-by-Step Geography). Danbury, CT: Children's Press, 1997.

Cumming, David. *Coasts* (Habitats). Austin, TX: Raintree Steck-Vaughn, 1997.

McLeish, Ewan. *Seas and Coasts* (Habitats). Austin, TX: Thomson Learning, 1996.

Neal, Philip. *The Oceans* (Conservation 2000). North Pomfret, VT: Trafalgar, 1993.

Multimedia

Exploring Water Habitats (Raintree Steck-Vaughn, 1997)

Internet sites

The Horsehead Wetlands Center Home Page can be found at http://www.covesoft.com/COVE/HTML/horsehead.html

Index